PASSWORD

LOG BOOK

NAME: _____

PHONE: _____

PASSWORD *Log*

🌐 Website	
👤 Login	
🔒 Password	
📄 Notes	

🌐 Website	
👤 Login	
🔒 Password	
📄 Notes	

🌐 Website	
👤 Login	
🔒 Password	
📄 Notes	

🌐 Website	
👤 Login	
🔒 Password	
📄 Notes	

PASSWORD *Log*

🌐 **Website**	
👤 **Login**	
🔒 **Password**	
🗊 **Notes**	

🌐 **Website**	
👤 **Login**	
🔒 **Password**	
🗊 **Notes**	

🌐 **Website**	
👤 **Login**	
🔒 **Password**	
🗊 **Notes**	

🌐 **Website**	
👤 **Login**	
🔒 **Password**	
🗊 **Notes**	

PASSWORD *Log*

🌐 Website	
👤 Login	
🔒 Password	
🗐 Notes	

🌐 Website	
👤 Login	
🔒 Password	
🗐 Notes	

🌐 Website	
👤 Login	
🔒 Password	
🗐 Notes	

🌐 Website	
👤 Login	
🔒 Password	
🗐 Notes	

PASSWORD *Log*

🌐 Website	
👤 Login	
🔒 Password	
📑 Notes	

🌐 Website	
👤 Login	
🔒 Password	
📑 Notes	

🌐 Website	
👤 Login	
🔒 Password	
📑 Notes	

🌐 Website	
👤 Login	
🔒 Password	
📑 Notes	

PASSWORD *Log*

B

🌐 Website	
👤 Login	
🔒 Password	
🗐 Notes	

🌐 Website	
👤 Login	
🔒 Password	
🗐 Notes	

🌐 Website	
👤 Login	
🔒 Password	
🗐 Notes	

🌐 Website	
👤 Login	
🔒 Password	
🗐 Notes	

PASSWORD *Log*

🌐 Website	
👤 Login	
🔒 Password	
🗒 Notes	

🌐 Website	
👤 Login	
🔒 Password	
🗒 Notes	

🌐 Website	
👤 Login	
🔒 Password	
🗒 Notes	

🌐 Website	
👤 Login	
🔒 Password	
🗒 Notes	

PASSWORD *Log*

🌐 Website	
👤 Login	
🔒 Password	
📋 Notes	

🌐 Website	
👤 Login	
🔒 Password	
📋 Notes	

🌐 Website	
👤 Login	
🔒 Password	
📋 Notes	

🌐 Website	
👤 Login	
🔒 Password	
📋 Notes	

PASSWORD *Log*

🌐 Website	
👤 Login	
🔒 Password	
📑 Notes	

🌐 Website	
👤 Login	
🔒 Password	
📑 Notes	

🌐 Website	
👤 Login	
🔒 Password	
📑 Notes	

🌐 Website	
👤 Login	
🔒 Password	
📑 Notes	

PASSWORD *Log*

C

🌐 **Website**	
👤 **Login**	
🔒 **Password**	
🗒 **Notes**	

🌐 **Website**	
👤 **Login**	
🔒 **Password**	
🗒 **Notes**	

🌐 **Website**	
👤 **Login**	
🔒 **Password**	
🗒 **Notes**	

🌐 **Website**	
👤 **Login**	
🔒 **Password**	
🗒 **Notes**	

PASSWORD *Log*

🌐 Website	
👤 Login	
🔒 Password	
📑 Notes	

🌐 Website	
👤 Login	
🔒 Password	
📑 Notes	

🌐 Website	
👤 Login	
🔒 Password	
📑 Notes	

🌐 Website	
👤 Login	
🔒 Password	
📑 Notes	

PASSWORD *Log*

C

🌐 **Website**	
👤 **Login**	
🔒 **Password**	
🗐 **Notes**	

🌐 **Website**	
👤 **Login**	
🔒 **Password**	
🗐 **Notes**	

🌐 **Website**	
👤 **Login**	
🔒 **Password**	
🗐 **Notes**	

🌐 **Website**	
👤 **Login**	
🔒 **Password**	
🗐 **Notes**	

PASSWORD *Log*

🌐 **Website**	
👤 **Login**	
🔒 **Password**	
🗐 **Notes**	

🌐 **Website**	
👤 **Login**	
🔒 **Password**	
🗐 **Notes**	

🌐 **Website**	
👤 **Login**	
🔒 **Password**	
🗐 **Notes**	

🌐 **Website**	
👤 **Login**	
🔒 **Password**	
🗐 **Notes**	

PASSWORD *Log*

🌐 Website	
👤 Login	
🔒 Password	
🗒 Notes	

🌐 Website	
👤 Login	
🔒 Password	
🗒 Notes	

🌐 Website	
👤 Login	
🔒 Password	
🗒 Notes	

🌐 Website	
👤 Login	
🔒 Password	
🗒 Notes	

PASSWORD *Log*

🌐 Website	
👤 Login	
🔒 Password	
🗒 Notes	

🌐 Website	
👤 Login	
🔒 Password	
🗒 Notes	

🌐 Website	
👤 Login	
🔒 Password	
🗒 Notes	

🌐 Website	
👤 Login	
🔒 Password	
🗒 Notes	

PASSWORD *Log*

D

🌐 **Website**	
👤 **Login**	
🔒 **Password**	
🗐 **Notes**	

🌐 **Website**	
👤 **Login**	
🔒 **Password**	
🗐 **Notes**	

🌐 **Website**	
👤 **Login**	
🔒 **Password**	
🗐 **Notes**	

🌐 **Website**	
👤 **Login**	
🔒 **Password**	
🗐 **Notes**	

PASSWORD *Log*

🌐 Website	
👤 Login	
🔒 Password	
🗐 Notes	

🌐 Website	
👤 Login	
🔒 Password	
🗐 Notes	

🌐 Website	
👤 Login	
🔒 Password	
🗐 Notes	

🌐 Website	
👤 Login	
🔒 Password	
🗐 Notes	

PASSWORD *Log*

E

🌐 **Website**	
👤 **Login**	
🔒 **Password**	
🗐 **Notes**	

🌐 **Website**	
👤 **Login**	
🔒 **Password**	
🗐 **Notes**	

🌐 **Website**	
👤 **Login**	
🔒 **Password**	
🗐 **Notes**	

🌐 **Website**	
👤 **Login**	
🔒 **Password**	
🗐 **Notes**	

PASSWORD *Log*

🌐 Website	
👤 Login	
🔒 Password	
📋 Notes	

🌐 Website	
👤 Login	
🔒 Password	
📋 Notes	

🌐 Website	
👤 Login	
🔒 Password	
📋 Notes	

🌐 Website	
👤 Login	
🔒 Password	
📋 Notes	

PASSWORD *Log*

E

🌐 Website	
👤 Login	
🔒 Password	
📒 Notes	

🌐 Website	
👤 Login	
🔒 Password	
📒 Notes	

🌐 Website	
👤 Login	
🔒 Password	
📒 Notes	

🌐 Website	
👤 Login	
🔒 Password	
📒 Notes	

PASSWORD *Log*

🌐 Website	
👤 Login	
🔒 Password	
📑 Notes	

🌐 Website	
👤 Login	
🔒 Password	
📑 Notes	

🌐 Website	
👤 Login	
🔒 Password	
📑 Notes	

🌐 Website	
👤 Login	
🔒 Password	
📑 Notes	

PASSWORD *Log*

F

🌐 Website	
👤 Login	
🔒 Password	
📝 Notes	

🌐 Website	
👤 Login	
🔒 Password	
📝 Notes	

🌐 Website	
👤 Login	
🔒 Password	
📝 Notes	

🌐 Website	
👤 Login	
🔒 Password	
📝 Notes	

PASSWORD *Log*

🌐 **Website**	
👤 **Login**	
🔒 **Password**	
🗐 **Notes**	

🌐 **Website**	
👤 **Login**	
🔒 **Password**	
🗐 **Notes**	

🌐 **Website**	
👤 **Login**	
🔒 **Password**	
🗐 **Notes**	

🌐 **Website**	
👤 **Login**	
🔒 **Password**	
🗐 **Notes**	

PASSWORD *Log*

F

🌐 Website	
👤 Login	
🔒 Password	
📋 Notes	

🌐 Website	
👤 Login	
🔒 Password	
📋 Notes	

🌐 Website	
👤 Login	
🔒 Password	
📋 Notes	

🌐 Website	
👤 Login	
🔒 Password	
📋 Notes	

PASSWORD *Log*

🌐 Website	
👤 Login	
🔒 Password	
🗊 Notes	

🌐 Website	
👤 Login	
🔒 Password	
🗊 Notes	

🌐 Website	
👤 Login	
🔒 Password	
🗊 Notes	

🌐 Website	
👤 Login	
🔒 Password	
🗊 Notes	

PASSWORD *Log*

G

🌐 Website	
👤 Login	
🔒 Password	
🗐 Notes	

🌐 Website	
👤 Login	
🔒 Password	
🗐 Notes	

🌐 Website	
👤 Login	
🔒 Password	
🗐 Notes	

🌐 Website	
👤 Login	
🔒 Password	
🗐 Notes	

PASSWORD *Log*

🌐 Website	
👤 Login	
🔒 Password	
🗐 Notes	

🌐 Website	
👤 Login	
🔒 Password	
🗐 Notes	

🌐 Website	
👤 Login	
🔒 Password	
🗐 Notes	

🌐 Website	
👤 Login	
🔒 Password	
🗐 Notes	

PASSWORD *Log*

🌐 Website	
👤 Login	
🔒 Password	
📝 Notes	

🌐 Website	
👤 Login	
🔒 Password	
📝 Notes	

🌐 Website	
👤 Login	
🔒 Password	
📝 Notes	

🌐 Website	
👤 Login	
🔒 Password	
📝 Notes	

PASSWORD *Log*

G

🌐 Website	
👤 Login	
🔒 Password	
🗒 Notes	

🌐 Website	
👤 Login	
🔒 Password	
🗒 Notes	

🌐 Website	
👤 Login	
🔒 Password	
🗒 Notes	

🌐 Website	
👤 Login	
🔒 Password	
🗒 Notes	

PASSWORD *Log*

H

🌐 Website	
👤 Login	
🔒 Password	
📋 Notes	

🌐 Website	
👤 Login	
🔒 Password	
📋 Notes	

🌐 Website	
👤 Login	
🔒 Password	
📋 Notes	

🌐 Website	
👤 Login	
🔒 Password	
📋 Notes	

PASSWORD *Log*

🌐 Website	
👤 Login	
🔒 Password	
🗊 Notes	

🌐 Website	
👤 Login	
🔒 Password	
🗊 Notes	

🌐 Website	
👤 Login	
🔒 Password	
🗊 Notes	

🌐 Website	
👤 Login	
🔒 Password	
🗊 Notes	

PASSWORD *Log*

H

🌐 **Website**	
👤 **Login**	
🔒 **Password**	
📇 **Notes**	

🌐 **Website**	
👤 **Login**	
🔒 **Password**	
📇 **Notes**	

🌐 **Website**	
👤 **Login**	
🔒 **Password**	
📇 **Notes**	

🌐 **Website**	
👤 **Login**	
🔒 **Password**	
📇 **Notes**	

PASSWORD *Log*

🌐 Website	
👤 Login	
🔒 Password	
📑 Notes	

🌐 Website	
👤 Login	
🔒 Password	
📑 Notes	

🌐 Website	
👤 Login	
🔒 Password	
📑 Notes	

🌐 Website	
👤 Login	
🔒 Password	
📑 Notes	

PASSWORD *Log*

🌐 **Website**	
👤 **Login**	
🔒 **Password**	
📑 **Notes**	

🌐 **Website**	
👤 **Login**	
🔒 **Password**	
📑 **Notes**	

🌐 **Website**	
👤 **Login**	
🔒 **Password**	
📑 **Notes**	

🌐 **Website**	
👤 **Login**	
🔒 **Password**	
📑 **Notes**	

PASSWORD *Log*

🌐 **Website**	
👤 **Login**	
🔒 **Password**	
🗐 **Notes**	

🌐 **Website**	
👤 **Login**	
🔒 **Password**	
🗐 **Notes**	

🌐 **Website**	
👤 **Login**	
🔒 **Password**	
🗐 **Notes**	

🌐 **Website**	
👤 **Login**	
🔒 **Password**	
🗐 **Notes**	

PASSWORD *Log*

🌐 **Website**	
👤 **Login**	
🔒 **Password**	
📓 **Notes**	

🌐 **Website**	
👤 **Login**	
🔒 **Password**	
📓 **Notes**	

🌐 **Website**	
👤 **Login**	
🔒 **Password**	
📓 **Notes**	

🌐 **Website**	
👤 **Login**	
🔒 **Password**	
📓 **Notes**	

PASSWORD *Log*

🌐 Website	
👤 Login	
🔒 Password	
🗒 Notes	

🌐 Website	
👤 Login	
🔒 Password	
🗒 Notes	

🌐 Website	
👤 Login	
🔒 Password	
🗒 Notes	

🌐 Website	
👤 Login	
🔒 Password	
🗒 Notes	

PASSWORD *Log*

J

🌐 **Website**	
👤 **Login**	
🔒 **Password**	
📋 **Notes**	

🌐 **Website**	
👤 **Login**	
🔒 **Password**	
📋 **Notes**	

🌐 **Website**	
👤 **Login**	
🔒 **Password**	
📋 **Notes**	

🌐 **Website**	
👤 **Login**	
🔒 **Password**	
📋 **Notes**	

PASSWORD *Log*

🌐 Website	
👤 Login	
🔒 Password	
📝 Notes	

🌐 Website	
👤 Login	
🔒 Password	
📝 Notes	

🌐 Website	
👤 Login	
🔒 Password	
📝 Notes	

🌐 Website	
👤 Login	
🔒 Password	
📝 Notes	

PASSWORD *Log*

J

🌐 **Website**	
👤 **Login**	
🔒 **Password**	
🗒 **Notes**	

🌐 **Website**	
👤 **Login**	
🔒 **Password**	
🗒 **Notes**	

🌐 **Website**	
👤 **Login**	
🔒 **Password**	
🗒 **Notes**	

🌐 **Website**	
👤 **Login**	
🔒 **Password**	
🗒 **Notes**	

PASSWORD *Log*

🌐 Website	
👤 Login	
🔒 Password	
📑 Notes	

🌐 Website	
👤 Login	
🔒 Password	
📑 Notes	

🌐 Website	
👤 Login	
🔒 Password	
📑 Notes	

🌐 Website	
👤 Login	
🔒 Password	
📑 Notes	

PASSWORD *Log*

K

🌐 Website	
👤 Login	
🔒 Password	
🗊 Notes	

🌐 Website	
👤 Login	
🔒 Password	
🗊 Notes	

🌐 Website	
👤 Login	
🔒 Password	
🗊 Notes	

🌐 Website	
👤 Login	
🔒 Password	
🗊 Notes	

PASSWORD *Log*

🌐 Website	
👤 Login	
🔒 Password	
📋 Notes	

🌐 Website	
👤 Login	
🔒 Password	
📋 Notes	

🌐 Website	
👤 Login	
🔒 Password	
📋 Notes	

🌐 Website	
👤 Login	
🔒 Password	
📋 Notes	

PASSWORD *Log*

K

🌐 Website	
👤 Login	
🔒 Password	
🗒 Notes	

🌐 Website	
👤 Login	
🔒 Password	
🗒 Notes	

🌐 Website	
👤 Login	
🔒 Password	
🗒 Notes	

🌐 Website	
👤 Login	
🔒 Password	
🗒 Notes	

PASSWORD *Log*

🌐 Website	
👤 Login	
🔒 Password	
🗒 Notes	

🌐 Website	
👤 Login	
🔒 Password	
🗒 Notes	

🌐 Website	
👤 Login	
🔒 Password	
🗒 Notes	

🌐 Website	
👤 Login	
🔒 Password	
🗒 Notes	

PASSWORD *Log*

L

🌐 Website	
👤 Login	
🔒 Password	
📋 Notes	

🌐 Website	
👤 Login	
🔒 Password	
📋 Notes	

🌐 Website	
👤 Login	
🔒 Password	
📋 Notes	

🌐 Website	
👤 Login	
🔒 Password	
📋 Notes	

PASSWORD *Log*

🌐 Website	
👤 Login	
🔒 Password	
🗒 Notes	

🌐 Website	
👤 Login	
🔒 Password	
🗒 Notes	

🌐 Website	
👤 Login	
🔒 Password	
🗒 Notes	

🌐 Website	
👤 Login	
🔒 Password	
🗒 Notes	

PASSWORD *Log*

L

🌐 **Website**	
👤 **Login**	
🔒 **Password**	
📋 **Notes**	

🌐 **Website**	
👤 **Login**	
🔒 **Password**	
📋 **Notes**	

🌐 **Website**	
👤 **Login**	
🔒 **Password**	
📋 **Notes**	

🌐 **Website**	
👤 **Login**	
🔒 **Password**	
📋 **Notes**	

PASSWORD *Log*

🌐 **Website**	
👤 **Login**	
🔒 **Password**	
🗒 **Notes**	

🌐 **Website**	
👤 **Login**	
🔒 **Password**	
🗒 **Notes**	

🌐 **Website**	
👤 **Login**	
🔒 **Password**	
🗒 **Notes**	

🌐 **Website**	
👤 **Login**	
🔒 **Password**	
🗒 **Notes**	

PASSWORD *Log*

M

🌐 **Website**	
👤 **Login**	
🔒 **Password**	
🗒 **Notes**	

🌐 **Website**	
👤 **Login**	
🔒 **Password**	
🗒 **Notes**	

🌐 **Website**	
👤 **Login**	
🔒 **Password**	
🗒 **Notes**	

🌐 **Website**	
👤 **Login**	
🔒 **Password**	
🗒 **Notes**	

PASSWORD *Log*

🌐 Website	
👤 Login	
🔒 Password	
🗒 Notes	

🌐 Website	
👤 Login	
🔒 Password	
🗒 Notes	

🌐 Website	
👤 Login	
🔒 Password	
🗒 Notes	

🌐 Website	
👤 Login	
🔒 Password	
🗒 Notes	

PASSWORD *Log*

M

🌐 **Website**	
👤 **Login**	
🔒 **Password**	
🗐 **Notes**	

🌐 **Website**	
👤 **Login**	
🔒 **Password**	
🗐 **Notes**	

🌐 **Website**	
👤 **Login**	
🔒 **Password**	
🗐 **Notes**	

🌐 **Website**	
👤 **Login**	
🔒 **Password**	
🗐 **Notes**	

PASSWORD *Log*

M

🌐 Website	
👤 Login	
🔒 Password	
📋 Notes	

🌐 Website	
👤 Login	
🔒 Password	
📋 Notes	

🌐 Website	
👤 Login	
🔒 Password	
📋 Notes	

🌐 Website	
👤 Login	
🔒 Password	
📋 Notes	

PASSWORD *Log*

N

🌐 **Website**	
👤 **Login**	
🔒 **Password**	
🗐 **Notes**	

🌐 **Website**	
👤 **Login**	
🔒 **Password**	
🗐 **Notes**	

🌐 **Website**	
👤 **Login**	
🔒 **Password**	
🗐 **Notes**	

🌐 **Website**	
👤 **Login**	
🔒 **Password**	
🗐 **Notes**	

PASSWORD *Log*

🌐 Website	
👤 Login	
🔒 Password	
📋 Notes	

🌐 Website	
👤 Login	
🔒 Password	
📋 Notes	

🌐 Website	
👤 Login	
🔒 Password	
📋 Notes	

🌐 Website	
👤 Login	
🔒 Password	
📋 Notes	

PASSWORD *Log*

N

🌐 Website	
👤 Login	
🔒 Password	
🗎 Notes	

🌐 Website	
👤 Login	
🔒 Password	
🗎 Notes	

🌐 Website	
👤 Login	
🔒 Password	
🗎 Notes	

🌐 Website	
👤 Login	
🔒 Password	
🗎 Notes	

PASSWORD *Log*

🌐 **Website**	
👤 **Login**	
🔒 **Password**	
📇 **Notes**	

🌐 **Website**	
👤 **Login**	
🔒 **Password**	
📇 **Notes**	

🌐 **Website**	
👤 **Login**	
🔒 **Password**	
📇 **Notes**	

🌐 **Website**	
👤 **Login**	
🔒 **Password**	
📇 **Notes**	

PASSWORD *Log*

🌐 Website	
👤 Login	
🔒 Password	
🗒 Notes	

🌐 Website	
👤 Login	
🔒 Password	
🗒 Notes	

🌐 Website	
👤 Login	
🔒 Password	
🗒 Notes	

🌐 Website	
👤 Login	
🔒 Password	
🗒 Notes	

PASSWORD *Log*

🌐 **Website**	
👤 **Login**	
🔒 **Password**	
🗐 **Notes**	

🌐 **Website**	
👤 **Login**	
🔒 **Password**	
🗐 **Notes**	

🌐 **Website**	
👤 **Login**	
🔒 **Password**	
🗐 **Notes**	

🌐 **Website**	
👤 **Login**	
🔒 **Password**	
🗐 **Notes**	

PASSWORD *Log*

0

🌐 **Website**	
👤 **Login**	
🔒 **Password**	
📝 **Notes**	

🌐 **Website**	
👤 **Login**	
🔒 **Password**	
📝 **Notes**	

🌐 **Website**	
👤 **Login**	
🔒 **Password**	
📝 **Notes**	

🌐 **Website**	
👤 **Login**	
🔒 **Password**	
📝 **Notes**	

PASSWORD *Log*

🌐 Website	
👤 Login	
🔒 Password	
🗒 Notes	

🌐 Website	
👤 Login	
🔒 Password	
🗒 Notes	

🌐 Website	
👤 Login	
🔒 Password	
🗒 Notes	

🌐 Website	
👤 Login	
🔒 Password	
🗒 Notes	

PASSWORD *Log*

P

🌐 Website	
👤 Login	
🔒 Password	
📋 Notes	

🌐 Website	
👤 Login	
🔒 Password	
📋 Notes	

🌐 Website	
👤 Login	
🔒 Password	
📋 Notes	

🌐 Website	
👤 Login	
🔒 Password	
📋 Notes	

PASSWORD *Log*

🌐 **Website**	
👤 **Login**	
🔒 **Password**	
🗐 **Notes**	

🌐 **Website**	
👤 **Login**	
🔒 **Password**	
🗐 **Notes**	

🌐 **Website**	
👤 **Login**	
🔒 **Password**	
🗐 **Notes**	

🌐 **Website**	
👤 **Login**	
🔒 **Password**	
🗐 **Notes**	

PASSWORD *Log*

🌐 **Website**	
👤 **Login**	
🔒 **Password**	
📋 **Notes**	

🌐 **Website**	
👤 **Login**	
🔒 **Password**	
📋 **Notes**	

🌐 **Website**	
👤 **Login**	
🔒 **Password**	
📋 **Notes**	

🌐 **Website**	
👤 **Login**	
🔒 **Password**	
📋 **Notes**	

PASSWORD *Log*

🌐 Website	
👤 Login	
🔒 Password	
🗐 Notes	

🌐 Website	
👤 Login	
🔒 Password	
🗐 Notes	

🌐 Website	
👤 Login	
🔒 Password	
🗐 Notes	

🌐 Website	
👤 Login	
🔒 Password	
🗐 Notes	

PASSWORD *Log*

Q

🌐 **Website**	
👤 **Login**	
🔒 **Password**	
🗒 **Notes**	

🌐 **Website**	
👤 **Login**	
🔒 **Password**	
🗒 **Notes**	

🌐 **Website**	
👤 **Login**	
🔒 **Password**	
🗒 **Notes**	

🌐 **Website**	
👤 **Login**	
🔒 **Password**	
🗒 **Notes**	

PASSWORD *Log*

🌐 **Website**	
👤 **Login**	
🔒 **Password**	
📋 **Notes**	

🌐 **Website**	
👤 **Login**	
🔒 **Password**	
📋 **Notes**	

🌐 **Website**	
👤 **Login**	
🔒 **Password**	
📋 **Notes**	

🌐 **Website**	
👤 **Login**	
🔒 **Password**	
📋 **Notes**	

PASSWORD *Log*

Q

🌐 **Website**	
👤 **Login**	
🔒 **Password**	
🗒 **Notes**	

🌐 **Website**	
👤 **Login**	
🔒 **Password**	
🗒 **Notes**	

🌐 **Website**	
👤 **Login**	
🔒 **Password**	
🗒 **Notes**	

🌐 **Website**	
👤 **Login**	
🔒 **Password**	
🗒 **Notes**	

PASSWORD *Log*

Q

🌐 **Website**	
👤 **Login**	
🔒 **Password**	
🗐 **Notes**	

🌐 **Website**	
👤 **Login**	
🔒 **Password**	
🗐 **Notes**	

🌐 **Website**	
👤 **Login**	
🔒 **Password**	
🗐 **Notes**	

🌐 **Website**	
👤 **Login**	
🔒 **Password**	
🗐 **Notes**	

PASSWORD *Log*

R

🌐 **Website**	
👤 **Login**	
🔒 **Password**	
📋 **Notes**	

🌐 **Website**	
👤 **Login**	
🔒 **Password**	
📋 **Notes**	

🌐 **Website**	
👤 **Login**	
🔒 **Password**	
📋 **Notes**	

🌐 **Website**	
👤 **Login**	
🔒 **Password**	
📋 **Notes**	

PASSWORD *Log*

🌐 **Website**	
👤 **Login**	
🔒 **Password**	
🗐 **Notes**	

🌐 **Website**	
👤 **Login**	
🔒 **Password**	
🗐 **Notes**	

🌐 **Website**	
👤 **Login**	
🔒 **Password**	
🗐 **Notes**	

🌐 **Website**	
👤 **Login**	
🔒 **Password**	
🗐 **Notes**	

PASSWORD *Log*

R

🌐 **Website**	
👤 **Login**	
🔒 **Password**	
🗒 **Notes**	

🌐 **Website**	
👤 **Login**	
🔒 **Password**	
🗒 **Notes**	

🌐 **Website**	
👤 **Login**	
🔒 **Password**	
🗒 **Notes**	

🌐 **Website**	
👤 **Login**	
🔒 **Password**	
🗒 **Notes**	

PASSWORD *Log*

R

🌐 Website	
👤 Login	
🔒 Password	
🗒 Notes	

🌐 Website	
👤 Login	
🔒 Password	
🗒 Notes	

🌐 Website	
👤 Login	
🔒 Password	
🗒 Notes	

🌐 Website	
👤 Login	
🔒 Password	
🗒 Notes	

PASSWORD *Log*

S

🌐 **Website**	
👤 **Login**	
🔒 **Password**	
📋 **Notes**	

🌐 **Website**	
👤 **Login**	
🔒 **Password**	
📋 **Notes**	

🌐 **Website**	
👤 **Login**	
🔒 **Password**	
📋 **Notes**	

🌐 **Website**	
👤 **Login**	
🔒 **Password**	
📋 **Notes**	

PASSWORD *Log*

🌐 Website	
👤 Login	
🔒 Password	
🗊 Notes	

🌐 Website	
👤 Login	
🔒 Password	
🗊 Notes	

🌐 Website	
👤 Login	
🔒 Password	
🗊 Notes	

🌐 Website	
👤 Login	
🔒 Password	
🗊 Notes	

PASSWORD *Log*

S

🌐 Website	
👤 Login	
🔒 Password	
📋 Notes	

🌐 Website	
👤 Login	
🔒 Password	
📋 Notes	

🌐 Website	
👤 Login	
🔒 Password	
📋 Notes	

🌐 Website	
👤 Login	
🔒 Password	
📋 Notes	

PASSWORD *Log*

🌐 Website	
👤 Login	
🔒 Password	
🗒 Notes	

🌐 Website	
👤 Login	
🔒 Password	
🗒 Notes	

🌐 Website	
👤 Login	
🔒 Password	
🗒 Notes	

🌐 Website	
👤 Login	
🔒 Password	
🗒 Notes	

PASSWORD *Log*

T

🌐 Website	
👤 Login	
🔒 Password	
🗎 Notes	

🌐 Website	
👤 Login	
🔒 Password	
🗎 Notes	

🌐 Website	
👤 Login	
🔒 Password	
🗎 Notes	

🌐 Website	
👤 Login	
🔒 Password	
🗎 Notes	

PASSWORD *Log*

T

🌍 **Website**	
👤 **Login**	
🔒 **Password**	
📇 **Notes**	

🌍 **Website**	
👤 **Login**	
🔒 **Password**	
📇 **Notes**	

🌍 **Website**	
👤 **Login**	
🔒 **Password**	
📇 **Notes**	

🌍 **Website**	
👤 **Login**	
🔒 **Password**	
📇 **Notes**	

PASSWORD *Log*

🌐 **Website**	
👤 **Login**	
🔒 **Password**	
🗈 **Notes**	

🌐 **Website**	
👤 **Login**	
🔒 **Password**	
🗈 **Notes**	

🌐 **Website**	
👤 **Login**	
🔒 **Password**	
🗈 **Notes**	

🌐 **Website**	
👤 **Login**	
🔒 **Password**	
🗈 **Notes**	

PASSWORD *Log*

🌐 Website	
👤 Login	
🔒 Password	
🗐 Notes	

🌐 Website	
👤 Login	
🔒 Password	
🗐 Notes	

🌐 Website	
👤 Login	
🔒 Password	
🗐 Notes	

🌐 Website	
👤 Login	
🔒 Password	
🗐 Notes	

PASSWORD *Log*

U

🌐 Website	
👤 Login	
🔒 Password	
📋 Notes	

🌐 Website	
👤 Login	
🔒 Password	
📋 Notes	

🌐 Website	
👤 Login	
🔒 Password	
📋 Notes	

🌐 Website	
👤 Login	
🔒 Password	
📋 Notes	

PASSWORD *Log*

🌐 Website	
👤 Login	
🔒 Password	
🗐 Notes	

🌐 Website	
👤 Login	
🔒 Password	
🗐 Notes	

🌐 Website	
👤 Login	
🔒 Password	
🗐 Notes	

🌐 Website	
👤 Login	
🔒 Password	
🗐 Notes	

PASSWORD *Log*

U

🌐 Website	
👤 Login	
🔒 Password	
🗒 Notes	

🌐 Website	
👤 Login	
🔒 Password	
🗒 Notes	

🌐 Website	
👤 Login	
🔒 Password	
🗒 Notes	

🌐 Website	
👤 Login	
🔒 Password	
🗒 Notes	

PASSWORD *Log*

🌐 **Website**	
👤 **Login**	
🔒 **Password**	
🗐 **Notes**	

🌐 **Website**	
👤 **Login**	
🔒 **Password**	
🗐 **Notes**	

🌐 **Website**	
👤 **Login**	
🔒 **Password**	
🗐 **Notes**	

🌐 **Website**	
👤 **Login**	
🔒 **Password**	
🗐 **Notes**	

PASSWORD *Log*

V

🌐 Website	
👤 Login	
🔒 Password	
📋 Notes	

🌐 Website	
👤 Login	
🔒 Password	
📋 Notes	

🌐 Website	
👤 Login	
🔒 Password	
📋 Notes	

🌐 Website	
👤 Login	
🔒 Password	
📋 Notes	

PASSWORD *Log*

🌐 **Website**	
👤 **Login**	
🔒 **Password**	
🗊 **Notes**	

🌐 **Website**	
👤 **Login**	
🔒 **Password**	
🗊 **Notes**	

🌐 **Website**	
👤 **Login**	
🔒 **Password**	
🗊 **Notes**	

🌐 **Website**	
👤 **Login**	
🔒 **Password**	
🗊 **Notes**	

PASSWORD *Log*

V

🌐 Website	
👤 Login	
🔒 Password	
🗐 Notes	

🌐 Website	
👤 Login	
🔒 Password	
🗐 Notes	

🌐 Website	
👤 Login	
🔒 Password	
🗐 Notes	

🌐 Website	
👤 Login	
🔒 Password	
🗐 Notes	

PASSWORD *Log*

🌐 Website	
👤 Login	
🔒 Password	
🗐 Notes	

🌐 Website	
👤 Login	
🔒 Password	
🗐 Notes	

🌐 Website	
👤 Login	
🔒 Password	
🗐 Notes	

🌐 Website	
👤 Login	
🔒 Password	
🗐 Notes	

PASSWORD *Log*

W

🌐 Website	
👤 Login	
🔒 Password	
📑 Notes	

🌐 Website	
👤 Login	
🔒 Password	
📑 Notes	

🌐 Website	
👤 Login	
🔒 Password	
📑 Notes	

🌐 Website	
👤 Login	
🔒 Password	
📑 Notes	

PASSWORD *Log*

🌐 Website	
👤 Login	
🔒 Password	
🗒 Notes	

🌐 Website	
👤 Login	
🔒 Password	
🗒 Notes	

🌐 Website	
👤 Login	
🔒 Password	
🗒 Notes	

🌐 Website	
👤 Login	
🔒 Password	
🗒 Notes	

PASSWORD *Log*

W

🌐 **Website**	
👤 **Login**	
🔒 **Password**	
🗐 **Notes**	

🌐 **Website**	
👤 **Login**	
🔒 **Password**	
🗐 **Notes**	

🌐 **Website**	
👤 **Login**	
🔒 **Password**	
🗐 **Notes**	

🌐 **Website**	
👤 **Login**	
🔒 **Password**	
🗐 **Notes**	

PASSWORD *Log*

🌐 Website	
👤 Login	
🔒 Password	
📝 Notes	

🌐 Website	
👤 Login	
🔒 Password	
📝 Notes	

🌐 Website	
👤 Login	
🔒 Password	
📝 Notes	

🌐 Website	
👤 Login	
🔒 Password	
📝 Notes	

PASSWORD *Log*

X

🌐 **Website**	
👤 **Login**	
🔒 **Password**	
🗐 **Notes**	

🌐 **Website**	
👤 **Login**	
🔒 **Password**	
🗐 **Notes**	

🌐 **Website**	
👤 **Login**	
🔒 **Password**	
🗐 **Notes**	

🌐 **Website**	
👤 **Login**	
🔒 **Password**	
🗐 **Notes**	

PASSWORD *Log*

X

🌐 Website	
👤 Login	
🔒 Password	
🗐 Notes	

🌐 Website	
👤 Login	
🔒 Password	
🗐 Notes	

🌐 Website	
👤 Login	
🔒 Password	
🗐 Notes	

🌐 Website	
👤 Login	
🔒 Password	
🗐 Notes	

PASSWORD *Log*

X

🌐 **Website**	
👤 **Login**	
🔒 **Password**	
🗊 **Notes**	

🌐 **Website**	
👤 **Login**	
🔒 **Password**	
🗊 **Notes**	

🌐 **Website**	
👤 **Login**	
🔒 **Password**	
🗊 **Notes**	

🌐 **Website**	
👤 **Login**	
🔒 **Password**	
🗊 **Notes**	

PASSWORD *Log*

X

🌐 Website	
👤 Login	
🔒 Password	
🗒 Notes	

🌐 Website	
👤 Login	
🔒 Password	
🗒 Notes	

🌐 Website	
👤 Login	
🔒 Password	
🗒 Notes	

🌐 Website	
👤 Login	
🔒 Password	
🗒 Notes	

PASSWORD *Log*

🌐 Website	
👤 Login	
🔒 Password	
🗊 Notes	

🌐 Website	
👤 Login	
🔒 Password	
🗊 Notes	

🌐 Website	
👤 Login	
🔒 Password	
🗊 Notes	

🌐 Website	
👤 Login	
🔒 Password	
🗊 Notes	

PASSWORD *Log*

🌐 Website	
👤 Login	
🔒 Password	
🗐 Notes	

🌐 Website	
👤 Login	
🔒 Password	
🗐 Notes	

🌐 Website	
👤 Login	
🔒 Password	
🗐 Notes	

🌐 Website	
👤 Login	
🔒 Password	
🗐 Notes	

PASSWORD *Log*

🌐 Website	
👤 Login	
🔒 Password	
📄 Notes	

🌐 Website	
👤 Login	
🔒 Password	
📄 Notes	

🌐 Website	
👤 Login	
🔒 Password	
📄 Notes	

🌐 Website	
👤 Login	
🔒 Password	
📄 Notes	

PASSWORD *Log*

🌐 Website	
👤 Login	
🔒 Password	
📓 Notes	

🌐 Website	
👤 Login	
🔒 Password	
📓 Notes	

🌐 Website	
👤 Login	
🔒 Password	
📓 Notes	

🌐 Website	
👤 Login	
🔒 Password	
📓 Notes	

PASSWORD *Log*

🌐 **Website**	
👤 **Login**	
🔒 **Password**	
🗐 **Notes**	

🌐 **Website**	
👤 **Login**	
🔒 **Password**	
🗐 **Notes**	

🌐 **Website**	
👤 **Login**	
🔒 **Password**	
🗐 **Notes**	

🌐 **Website**	
👤 **Login**	
🔒 **Password**	
🗐 **Notes**	

PASSWORD *Log*

🌐 Website	
👤 Login	
🔒 Password	
📋 Notes	

🌐 Website	
👤 Login	
🔒 Password	
📋 Notes	

🌐 Website	
👤 Login	
🔒 Password	
📋 Notes	

🌐 Website	
👤 Login	
🔒 Password	
📋 Notes	

PASSWORD *Log*

🌐 **Website**	
👤 **Login**	
🔒 **Password**	
🗒 **Notes**	

🌐 **Website**	
👤 **Login**	
🔒 **Password**	
🗒 **Notes**	

🌐 **Website**	
👤 **Login**	
🔒 **Password**	
🗒 **Notes**	

🌐 **Website**	
👤 **Login**	
🔒 **Password**	
🗒 **Notes**	

PASSWORD *Log*

🌐 Website	
👤 Login	
🔒 Password	
📋 Notes	

🌐 Website	
👤 Login	
🔒 Password	
📋 Notes	

🌐 Website	
👤 Login	
🔒 Password	
📋 Notes	

🌐 Website	
👤 Login	
🔒 Password	
📋 Notes	

PASSWORD *Log*

Z

🌐 Website	
👤 Login	
🔒 Password	
🗐 Notes	

🌐 Website	
👤 Login	
🔒 Password	
🗐 Notes	

🌐 Website	
👤 Login	
🔒 Password	
🗐 Notes	

🌐 Website	
👤 Login	
🔒 Password	
🗐 Notes	

Made in the USA
Monee, IL
22 August 2022